My Role in Healing After Betrayal

By Shanna Foster

In memory of my grandmother Edaphnie
Pettigrew (1927-2025)

Her strength and legacy of faith live on in these
pages.

Thank you to my Lord, Jehovah-Rapha, for his
love, grace and faithfulness.

ISBN: 979-8-9952492-1-4 (Paperback)

ISBN: 979-8-9952492-0-7 (E-Book)

Scripture quotations marked NIV are from the New International Version
First Edition: April 2026

Printed in the United States
Published by Shanna N Foster
Mahopac, NY

Table of Contents

Chapter 1

Preface - Why Write a Book?

My desire for writing this book stems from a passion to help others navigate and heal from betrayal. I want to be the woman who can walk through hell but still comes out carrying water for others. I want to help others extinguish the flames of betrayal faster than they might on their own. Most importantly, I want to show others how to come out stronger than before.

This book is for the woman enduring the pain of being betrayed or abandoned by a spouse, family member, or friend. This is for the woman who is struggling to get out of bed in the morning. Pain is pain regardless of what caused it. I know the feeling of endless tears, profound sadness, and unbearable pain that can bring you to the point of begging for death. I pray this book makes you feel seen, fills you with hope, and helps you to quickly get your footing on the path to healing.

Unfortunately, I've endured this kind of pain multiple times in my life. Each time I made the decision to learn as much as I could from others and find a way to healing and purpose. As you read this book, I encourage you to highlight, underline, or bookmark anything that resonates with you. You'll want to revisit those sections. I've kept a journal for the past 10 years, documenting all the lessons I've learned and applied. Anytime I read or hear something impactful, I underline it and then write it in my journal. I call these my Ah-Ha moments, and they're all written in one place. I revisit the lessons I've learned over the years, and they renew and refresh me. It helps me remember what I've learned and continually put it into practice. All of which have led to miraculous healing and a great sense of purpose in my life.

I am a woman of Christian faith, and this book is written with both a faith-based lens on healing and proven scientific methods for healing through the brain. It contains all the lessons I've learned during the painful years, as I desperately searched for answers of hope. I'll be sharing actionable advice you can put into practice over an extended period. These are not one-time-and-you're-done actions. Healing takes time, but it can be quicker if you're intentional about what you do with this period of time in your life.

Chapter 2

Early Days after Betrayal

The Shock Phase:

My story comes from a betrayal by my spouse. I can still remember the initial period of shock. I was in shock for several weeks. I remember just staring into space for hours, unable to move and feeling paralyzed by unbearable pain. I was paralyzed to the point that I couldn't find the words to pray. All I could get out was "Jesus," and that was my only prayer for quite some time. Just a one-word prayer. But I knew it was enough in those moments. I wasn't alone as long as I cried out to Jesus. I remember the weeks of constant nausea, vomiting, chest pains, and scary panic attacks; where it wasn't clear if I needed to call an ambulance due to an actual heart attack. I remember uncontrollably crying anytime, anywhere, anyplace. This meant breaking down in stores, parking lots, the shower, and in the quiet moments of the night. I remember thinking I'll never be able to ever smile again.

If you're in this initial phase of shock after any type of betrayal, my first piece of advice is to tell someone you trust. The last thing you want to do is isolate yourself. Choose someone who will not gossip. Choose someone who will encourage and check on you. Choose someone that you know when they say they're praying for you, you know they're really going home and praying for you. This was key for me. I told a few close friends who genuinely prayed for me and with me. They made time to sit with me, chat on the phone, help watch the kids, and do anything to make life a bit easier. Surround yourself with the kind of women who want the best for you and will drop everything to be there when you need them. These women were instrumental in helping me come out of the initial shock phase.

After The Shock Phase:

At this point, I started to remember who I was as a child of God and that He doesn't stop being the Lord of my life because of my circumstances. This started my healing journey: my burning desire to learn, biblically, how to handle these painful moments in life and how God wants me to respond. I asked the Lord, "what is my role in my own healing, according to Your Word"? I spent the next several years digging into the Word, listening to thousands of hours of sermons, podcasts, and reading countless books on healing, trauma, and betrayal. This is how I received all the "Ah-Ha" moments captured in my journal. I plan to share everything I learned about my role in my own healing and what actually worked. If you can apply some of the lessons in this book, you will be filled with hope for the future and not remain consumed by pain or bitterness.

The first thing I did was sign up for a daily devotional for women, which was emailed to me every morning.   I would read the email before getting out of bed. It only took about 5 minutes, but it set the tone for my day. It made it easier on the days when the pain made it hard to get out of bed.   Starting my day in the Word uplifted me and renewed my strength.

The second thing I did was sign up for an online support group. You can do a quick Google search for support groups specific to the type of trauma or betrayal you're going through. There are tons of free online support groups, both faith-based and non-faith-based. I found it helpful to read others' experiences and realize that my emotions and responses were normal. Personally, I'm more on the quiet side, so I didn't post much, but I gained a lot just by reading through the posts every day. The group became a source of encouragement and hope. If you're able to find an in-person support group, that's even better. The group I joined had a mix of people still in the initial shock phase and people a few years out. Everyone had their own perspectives and insights to share. Being a part of a community that truly understands what you're going through and is currently walking in your same shoes makes each day a little less lonely.

Next, I signed up for free Podcasts. I started following several podcasts, both faith-based and non-faith-based, that discussed betrayal and trauma. This also included podcasts from preachers and sermons about everyday life as a Christian. I didn't want to just learn about how to heal God's way; I wanted to learn how to draw closer to the Lord. I wanted to learn how to be the best bride for Christ in every area of my life. Whatever I was learning in the podcasts, I would then look up what the Bible actually had to say. You want to make sure you're not just going by what you hear, you want to read it for yourself directly in the Bible. This is how I really started to grow in wisdom and gain revelations on how I needed to apply the lessons to my specific circumstances.

Lastly, I read as many books as I could find by authors who had gone through my same circumstances and had successfully navigated to find healing. One of my favorite authors during this time was Lysa TerKeurst. I learned a lot of valuable lessons from her.

So now you know everything I did very early on to start learning the best way to move forward. For several years, I continued to read the devotional, stayed in the support group, listened to the podcasts, read the Bible and other books with a fire and desperation. I look back now, and this was my way of distracting myself from the pain. In the next chapters, I'll share the life-changing lessons I learned in those years and how I applied them. The key is that you have to actually live what you've learned. I don't have the best memory, which is why I wrote the lessons in a journal. I don't want you to just read this book and then forget most of what you read. Please invest in yourself and write down anything that stands out to you; anything you want to remember and incorporate into your life.

Chapter 3

Why did this happen?

Asking "Why" and the overwhelming need to have an answer to "Why", is human nature. We believe that if we could just understand why this happened, it would help us process it better. In reality, understanding why doesn't take the pain away. It may lessen it, but it doesn't remove it. My desire to understand why is what drove me to start my research on pain and what the Bible has to say about it. Here, I'll share everything I learned about why we have hardships.

Turns out the main answer to why was one simple word: Sin. Most of life's tough moments happen because of sin. I say "most" because there are also times when God allows tough moments to teach us and for His Glory to be revealed. I found there are 3 categories of what causes the painful moments in our lives: The sins of others, our own sins, and trials God allows to grow us.

Sin of Others

A good example here is adultery. If your spouse commits adultery, there are natural consequences that come along with that sin. This causes extremely painful moments in your life and the lives of other family members, such as children. It's a ripple effect that devastates multiple people who never asked to be involved. Any type of betrayal in our lives is caused by someone else's sin.

Our Own Sin

A good example here is pornography. Most people are fooled into believing that this is a hidden sin that doesn't impact anyone else. Every hidden sin will eventually come to light and harm those closest to us. There are natural consequences here, too. With the pornography example, it can change how you treat and view your partner. It can also give you unrealistic expectations of sex from your partner. This can seriously damage a marriage. Another example here is lying. Do not fall for the trap of believing that lying only impacts the ones speaking the lies. Every lie will eventually be exposed and shatter trust. When trust is broken, it takes years to earn back. We need to be in constant self-reflection to ensure we don't have secret sins that will destroy our relationships with loved ones. We all need to be cognizant of how our own sin will impact those we love.

God Allows Trials

During my years of studying, I read the story of the blind man in the book of John. I've heard this story a hundred times before, but it struck me differently this time.

₁ As he went along, he saw a man blind from birth. ₂ His disciples asked Him, "Rabbi, who sinned, this man or his parents, that he was born blind?" ₃ "Neither this man nor his parents sinned," said Jesus, "but this happened so that the works of God might be displayed in him. ₄ As long as it is day, we must do the work of the one who sent me. Night is coming, when no one can work. ₅ While I am in the world, I am the light of the world." ₆ After saying this, he spit on the ground, made some mud with the saliva, and put it on the man's eyes. ₇ "Go," he told him, "Wash in the Pool of Siloam". So, the man went and washed, and came home seeing.

I had always glazed over the part where Jesus says neither this man nor his parents sinned. He had been blind his entire life from birth. He endured hardships throughout his life, and it wasn't because of sin. Jesus goes on to say that he was blind so that the works of God would be displayed in his life. The Lord allowed the suffering so he could be miraculously healed for others to witness and be encouraged in their faith. God's mighty works were on display not just for those in that period of time but for all ages. We're still reading the blind man's story thousands of years later. God used his life in a mighty way. His story continues to bring hope today and reveal God's Glory.

This new understanding of the blind man made me reflect on my own life. I'll share that I was born severely deformed in both feet. Throughout my life, I've had multiple surgeries, mostly reconstructive, to give me the ability to walk. I'll always have struggles and pain, but I'm thankful I have the freedom to be able to walk at all. I used to question why God would have allowed this to happen to me. I'll never be able to run a marathon, wear high heels, or stand on my tippy toes to reach something on a high shelf. As a child, I definitely had resentment towards the

Lord for why I had to be physically different from everyone else.

After my new revelation of the blind man's story, I believe there's a possibility my deformity happened so God could get the Glory. I don't know that for sure, but it's also possible that there was sin in my parents' lives that caused this. But if God allowed it, I choose to live a life that gives Him Glory. Also, when you live with a physical ailment, it can develop certain characteristics in you and a specific personality. It can give you a unique position of being able to minister to others in a way you may not have otherwise. I can remember being in school and always gravitating to those who were singled out for being different or had trouble making friends. Since I knew how it felt to be different, it developed in me a heart to help others. I was a friend to the friendless and sought out those who I could tell were hurting. That compassion developed in me because of my physical ailments. 40 years later, I still have that deep compassion to help others, and God will get the Glory in all I do.

The blind man's story may be an extreme example of when God allows suffering for a purpose. Things like abuse or betrayals are always because of sin and not of God. If you're going through a difficult time and you can't make a direct connection to sin, you should ask yourself if it could be a trial meant to grow you, equip you, and make you stronger. The purpose of the trial may be to develop the characteristics you need for your calling.

This led me to learning the difference between temptations and trials. I guess I always thought these had the same meaning, but they're different in the Bible. I can usually trace a lot of the uncomfortable moments of life to a temptation or a trial. Being aware of the difference helps you respond appropriately.

Temptation is an invitation to sin. It's a pull to evil that interrupts our spiritual growth. Temptation is only a sin once you act on it. The enemy tempts us, the world tempts us, and our flesh tempts us. God will provide an exit. An example would be lust and the desire to watch pornography or commit adultery. Temptation is like a lure pulling you to disobey God. The book of Matthew teaches that all will experience temptation.

Matthews 18:7 NIV

> *7 Woe to the world because of the things that cause people to stumble! Such things must come, but woe to the person through whom they come!*

Trials are different from temptation. Trials grow us spiritually. For instance, you may lose your job, which can be scary, but God has another one lined up. He's teaching you to rely on Him and build your faith. Trials are tests to grow you in certain areas, like patience. If you're someone who struggles with patience, then you'll probably face situations that will test your patience or self-control. The only way to grow in that area is to face difficulties and practice being patient until it comes naturally.

James 1:12 NIV

12 Blessed is the one who perseveres under trial because, having stood the test, that person will receive the crown of life that the Lord has promised to those who love Him.

Hebrews 12:11 NIV

11 No discipline seems pleasant at the time, but painful. Later on, however, it produces a harvest of righteousness and peace for those who have been trained by it.

Here are the key differences between a temptation and a trial: The difference is in the source and outcome. Temptation's source is a lie from the enemy and our own selfish desires. The outcome leads to destruction. Temptation never comes from God, which I've found to be a big misconception. We should never say God is tempting us.

James 1:13 NIV

> *13 When tempted, no one should say, "God is tempting me." For God cannot be tempted by evil, nor does He tempt anyone;*

A trial's source comes from God, and they're teachable moments, not meant to cause destruction. The outcome is a truth we learn to apply in our lives. I didn't want to hear this, but trials can be both painful and a gift. It comes from a place of Godly love to bring us to new heights in our walk with the Lord. It's preparing us for our calling and new seasons that require us to master certain qualities.

I remember thanking God for showing me so much about why we go through hardships. I was also questioning why He waited until I was in such a painful season to pour these lessons into me. I feel we tend to learn and grow the most during the painful times of life. I asked the Lord why He waits to grow us in these moments because it doesn't seem fair. I actually got an answer to that question immediately. I felt something in me ask, "Did you seek Me this desperately when everything was good?" Of course, the answer was "No". The Lord was able to teach me more during this time after the betrayal because I was desperately seeking Him and spending hours in the Word. I don't spend this kind of time pursuing Him when everything is fine. At that moment, I understood He could pour into me like that at any time. It depends on how much I invest in our relationship and how much I choose to seek Him. We don't need to wait till we're desperate and in pain to cry out for more of God. We can cry out to God in the good times, cry out in gratitude and thankfulness.

Now, having a better understanding of why certain events occur in our lives, I know the Word does say that God can use all of it for our good. No matter the root cause, He can use it and weave it together to bring good in your life. He promises to redeem what we've endured.

Romans 8:28 NIV

> 28 *And we know that in all things God works for the good of those who love Him, who have been called according to His purpose.*

Chapter 4

My Role in Healing: Prayer and Thanksgiving

Philippians 4:6-7 NIV

> *6 Do not be anxious about anything, but in every situation, by prayer and petition, with thanksgiving, present your requests to God. 7 And the peace of God, which transcends all understanding, will guard your hearts and your minds in Christ Jesus.*

A strong prayer life is key for healing. Some think a strong prayer life means long, drawn-out prayers. But it's more about your heart, and that could mean praying for a few minutes or a few hours.

After a few weeks of my one-word prayer "Jesus", I began praying for myself, my children, and my husband. I found tons of online resources for marriage restoration prayers, prayers over your spouse, and prayers of healing for yourself. You can easily find prayers regarding betrayals by friends, family, or church members. I encourage you to find a few sample prayers tailored to your situation and save them in a place where they're easily accessible. You need to be consistent in your daily prayer, especially in moments of needing healing. It's how you keep your eyes fixed on the Lord.

One thing I learned is that you should always start your prayers with thanksgiving. We can't forget that there are still good things in our lives even during the storms. Think about how much worse things would feel if you also didn't have hot water, electricity, or food to eat. Or if you also lost your ability to see, hear, or walk. Each of these are blessings in our lives. Before you start asking the Lord for help with what you need, first thank Him for all the blessings. Ask yourself whether there are comforts in my life that I take for granted and need to thank the Lord for.

This lesson of thanksgiving is one I actually learned in a very powerful way as a child. I had an encounter with the Lord that forever shaped the personality that I still have today. I mentioned in an earlier chapter that I was born with deformities in both feet. That meant I walked differently from all the other children in elementary school. Being different feels like the end of the world as a child because children can be blunt and cruel. In addition, I was one of only two black children in an all-white school. Several of my kindergarten classmates asked to move their seats out of fear someone with my skin color would accidentally touch them. On top of that, I was being raised by my grandmother, not my parents. I was the only child who didn't live with their parents, which was foreign to everyone else. Needless to say, I felt so different that it was like being the only elephant in a room full of mice, everywhere I went. I just longed to fit in and be another mouse blending in with all the other mice.

After years of feeling this way, it started to build a resentment in me towards the Lord. At the age of 13, I realized I could never wear high heels because of all the surgeries, and that was the straw that broke the camel's back. Any teenage girl knows how serious high heels are. I decided I was done with the Lord, and either He didn't exist or He was just cruel.

That week, as my grandmother was taking my sister and me to church, we passed a funeral procession on the Southern State Parkway in Long Island, NY. A question popped into my head and asked, what do you think the family in that funeral procession would pay if they could buy your life's circumstances? What if they could pay to buy my circumstance of being an innocent bystander, not in a funeral procession, but about to get off the highway? What if they could buy my circumstance of being ignorant of the pain of losing a loved one? I thought they would probably give every cent, empty their bank account or sell their home if it meant they still had everyone alive, as I did in my life. The next question I heard was, would they still buy your circumstances if they knew it came along with all the foot surgeries? I thought yes. If the family in that funeral procession lost a child or spouse, then yes, I believe they would still buy my circumstances if it meant their loved one was alive, as all of mine were. The questions kept coming. What about all the people in the world where surgery was not an option for them to be able to walk, or anyone who had lost their sight, would they buy your circumstances if it meant they could walk or see? Probably yes. It hit me, if there are folks who would be willing to give

"Everything" to have my life, then that meant I already had "Everything".

I realized that the abundant life I kept hearing about in church was already mine. I just couldn't see it or feel it because I allowed my circumstances to blind me. I asked the Lord to forgive me, and it was like veils were removed from my eyes.

2 Corinthians 3:16-18 NIV

16 But whenever anyone turns to the Lord, the veil is taken away. 17 Now the Lord is the Spirit, and where the Spirit of the Lord is, there is freedom. 18 And we all, who with unveiled faces contemplate the Lord's Glory, are being transformed into his image with ever-increasing Glory, which comes from the Lord, who is the Spirit.

I could clearly see all the things I took for granted when I should've had a thankful heart.

One of the biggest things I missed was why I ended up living with my grandmother. She was a retired pediatric nurse who lived alone and had the time and living space to care for my sister and me. Can you imagine the number of circumstances the Lord was aligning going back 30 years prior, when she first even had a thought to be a pediatric nurse? He aligned things so I would be taken care of by someone who knew how to tend to my surgery wounds. He prepared her to be able to give me years of free physical therapy, which is why I didn't end up in a wheelchair. Not only did He send her to provide for all my physical needs, but also my spiritual needs.

My grandmother was a woman of strong faith. At age 4, she taught me how to play the piano so we could worship as a family. She taught me how to pray, read, and meditate on scripture. She left a legacy of faith woven into the fabric of who I am. My 13-year-old self realized that high heels were not part of His concerns for me to live a fully blessed life. My desire for materialistic things died that day, and I've lived a minimalistic life ever since. The abundant life is about the Lord meeting all your spiritual and physical needs. That needs to be enough for us to shout out with Thanksgiving. A grateful heart is a heart that can heal much faster than one that's not.

This revelation gave me the peaceful temperament I still have 30-plus years later. It takes a lot to get me upset because I can still recognize what's most important. I try to find at least one thing to be thankful for each day. It's a practice I do especially during the most painful moments. I increased this practice during the early pains after betrayal. I can say thank you, Lord, for the eyesight to see 2 squirrels chasing each other. Thank you, Lord, that I have the freedom to get up and walk where I please. Thank you, Jesus, that I can hear my son's sweet voice singing in the shower. I challenge you to find small moments of gratitude every day and thank God for them at the start of every prayer.

A lot of life's annoyances just don't really matter in the grand scheme. I also realized that we were not meant to blend in with everyone else. I was always supposed to be the elephant in the room because I walked with the Lord. We're supposed to be different and set apart so others can be drawn to Him, in us, and we can share our testimonies. If there's something you don't like about yourself because it makes you feel different, ask the Lord to help you make peace with it. He can use those differences to make you stand out and pull others to you. These differences can be what makes us the perfect person to minister to others. Today, I'm able to say thank you, Jesus, that I'm different because of You. That's enough

for me to give thanks until my last breath.

Chapter 5

My Role in Healing: Obedience and Faith

If you want to heal quickly, then obedience and faith also need to come into play. Increasing your faith comes by reading the Word and through obedience. When you spend time reading about the miracles in the Bible, it helps grow your faith. You get an understanding of who God is and how He responds in different situations. We see examples of His faithfulness and all He accomplished in various lives. It builds my faith when I read about women who remained faithful and how God blessed their obedience. I believe the same God that parted the sea is the same God I serve today, and that increases my faith.

We also need to have faith in His timing, especially when it comes to healing. Healing can't happen instantly. Use this time in your life to let

God pour into you all that's needed for your next season. I remember at one point crying out to God to please take the pain away instantly. I knew He could. But instead, it took several years. But over those years, I learned more than all my years prior. What I learned during that time is why I'm able to write this book. It's why I'm able to teach Bible Studies through my church. The best of all is that I was able to help other women get through their trauma. The Lord has placed over 50 women in my path over the years so I've been able to share what I've learned and help them heal or restore their marriages. I shudder to think of what could've happened if He had answered my prayer of impatience to be healed in my timing. If He had healed me instantly, I would not have desperately sought Him out during those years. I wouldn't have known what to say or how to help any of the women who crossed my path. It's scary to think of the amount of destruction that could have happened if my healing had happened in my timing instead of His perfect timing.

Let's talk about faith. Faith means both believing beyond what we see or feel and trusting His timing. In addition to reading the word, faith is also built by obedience. Every time we step out in faith, we see that He's faithful. Each time we see He's faithful, we realize that we can trust Him with bigger things. Without obedience, our faith is meaningless. We can say we have faith, but if we're not willing to take the steps of action and trust God, we really don't have any faith.

James 2:14-17 NIV

14 What good is it, my brothers and sisters, if someone claims to have faith but has no deeds? Can such faith save them? 15 Suppose a brother or a sister is without clothes and daily food. 16 If one of you says to them, "Go in peace; keep warm and well fed," but does nothing about their physical needs, what good is it? 17 In the same way, faith by itself, if it is not accompanied by action, is dead.

In other words, our faith needs to show in our walk, not just our talk. It means choosing to obey even when it doesn't make sense or when things seem impossible. As we step into faith, our faith increases. Start by trusting God with small things and see how He comes through. This reminds me of the mustard seed. A mustard seed is an extremely tiny seed that can grow into a 15-foot tree. Our faith starts out small as well, but every time we're obedient and see how He takes care of us, it grows our faith little by little. Until eventually our faith grows to the 15-foot tree, where we have the kind of faith that moves mountains; the kind of faith where you can still have peace while healing from betrayal or trauma. This doesn't mean you won't have pain, tears or fears, but it does mean you have a hope inside that you know everything will work for good, and you will see the light of day again. That's called the joy of the Lord, which we'll look at more closely in a further chapter.

Faith also means we can't comprehend God through the lens of our trauma. Sometimes we tend to direct our feelings for the person who hurt us towards God. We can begin to feel doubt and anger, wondering if God is even there or cares. I'm here to remind you that God's character doesn't change, no matter what we're going through. His promises aren't cancelled because of our circumstances. Allow God to grow your faith with each step of obedience.

Chapter 6

My Role in Healing: Forgiveness and Love

I remember feeling like forgiveness was the last thing I wanted to hear about. How do you forgive someone who has caused such crippling pain in your life? The key here is asking the Lord to help you see this person as He does and to help you respond to this person as He would. This is where knowing what the Bible says is helpful. You need to understand what kind of person Jesus was and how He saw everyone around Him. Then we can ask for the grace and wisdom to respond as Jesus would.

So, what kind of person was Jesus? He was the embodiment of forgiveness because He recognized the root of people's behaviors. He knew that sin and ignorance cause people to behave cruelly without knowing they're under a dark influence. He could see the invisible bondage someone was in that caused them to hurt others. You've probably heard the old saying "hurt people, hurt people". It's not just a cliche; it's spot on. This is why Jesus was able to say in Luke 23:34, "Father, forgive them, for they do not know what they are doing," as He was about to die at their hands.

Forgiveness means being able to look past the physical person and see them through a spiritual lens. Once you're able to do that, you can understand that the issue is within them and not within you. Once I was able to look at things this way, it made it easier for me to pray for my spouse. I understood that the best possible thing I could do is pray for Godly characteristics to build in him. When God commands us to forgive and pray, it's more for our benefit than theirs. I've had a lot of people ask how I could pray for someone who has hurt me so much. Why would you wish for anything good to happen to them?

My response is that I'm not praying for the person to win the lottery or win a new car. I'm praying for God's will and character for this person. When you can get to a place of genuinely praying for someone who hurt you, it will free you. Not only is this freeing and healing, but it's your best weapon to protect yourself from getting hurt further. If, through your prayers, God gets a hold of this person's heart, they won't be capable of harming anyone any further.

Holding on to unforgiveness will leave you stuck in the pain, and then bitterness will take root. We also need to let go of feelings of revenge or hate. Hurting someone back will not bring healing. It will do the complete opposite. Letting go of bitterness or hate frees up space in our hearts for healing. This can be especially difficult if you never get the apology, you desperately want to hear or see any change in behavior. We have to make peace with the fact that we may never get those things, even if it's what we deserve. Forgiveness has to be in spite of how the other person handles themself.

Pray daily and ask for help in this area. If you truly don't want to hinder your healing, you'll have to make this a daily decision. If you want freedom from the pain and faster progress on healing, then you'll need to forgive. Choosing to forgive, especially when it's hard, is the kind of obedience that will unlock heaven in your life.

I had a revelation around the story of David. In the book of Acts, it says that David was a man after God's own heart, but he's also someone who committed adultery and murder. If he could fall so far into sin, then I'm susceptible too. None of us is better than David and can fall into sin if we don't guard our hearts and minds. If I'm susceptible to sin, then so is everyone else. Meditating on that made it a little easier to choose forgiveness.

Acts 13:22 NIV

> 22 *After removing Saul, He made David their king. God testified concerning him: 'I have found David, son of Jesse, a man after my own heart; he will do everything I want him to do.'*

The most important reason for forgiving is that you want your Father in heaven to forgive you too. There's no one on this planet worth giving up eternity for because you didn't want to forgive. It's just not worth it.

Matthew 6:15 NIV

> 15 *But if you do not forgive others their sins, your Father will not forgive your sins.*

Along with forgiveness, we're also commanded to love. They go hand in hand. Choosing to forgive is an act of love, especially when paired with praying for that person. To be honest, this was the hardest thing for me to do. Choosing to love when you don't feel like it, but out of obedience to the Lord, is difficult. But I was determined to handle things God's way and not my own, so I started researching how to choose to love those who are hard to love.

Choosing to love means showing love in the quiet moments of life when no one is watching, as well as showing love for others to see. It means when that person isn't in the room, you still choose to love even if they may never see it. It's about choosing what you let your mind dwell on. It's about what's truly in your heart. You can pretend to love someone outwardly, but if in your heart and mind you're festering hatred or bitterness, it will eventually reveal itself. Obedience is more about what's hidden inside.

I remember a time when I went to change out the dirty bath towels hanging in the bathroom and replace them with clean ones. I remembered we had one towel that was always rough and coarse. No matter how much fabric softener I used, I couldn't get it to be any softer. When this particular towel came to mind, I searched for it and decided that's the one I'm giving my husband this week. He would have no clue it was done on purpose. He would have no clue it was placed there maliciously. Not only would he not know, but no one else would know either. As I walked toward the bathroom, towel in hand, I suddenly stopped. I asked myself, "Is this God's way or my way?" and I was brought back to the promise I had made myself to do it His way.

It's in these quiet moments of obedience that God can use mightily because it takes strength to obey when no one is looking. It takes strength to do the right thing when no one is there to applaud or outwardly praise you in front of others. This is where real Godly character is built. I immediately put the towel back and actually gave him our best towel. Then I asked the Lord's forgiveness and thanked Him for His grace, strength, and will to handle my healing His way. In hindsight, I can see all the miracles and supernatural healing that birthed out of those quiet moments of obedience.

Now, this towel example may sound like a silly one that doesn't mean much, but you'd be wrong. This is where we get ensnared in a trap. We believe these small moments, where no one is watching, will have no impact. That's a very slippery slope that will embolden you to make bigger, hidden acts each time you think no one saw. The Lord can't do the work in us if we're choosing to do things that keep us stuck and hinder our progress.

Here's something I practice and recommend. I know that there's a certain amount of satisfaction that comes from acting out in revenge, spite, or malice. It feels good for a moment to get back at someone or momentarily inflict the same pain they imposed on you. But those moments of satisfaction are fleeting and are often followed by guilt or shame. I have made a practice of asking myself, which do I want more: A momentary satisfaction or an eternal, everlasting satisfaction of knowing the Lord is saying, "Well done, my good and faithful servant". You can guess which one wins every time. One of these reactions reminds you that the wound is still raw, and the other reaction brings healing. This means training yourself not to act on impulse but to pause and weigh the consequences of how you're about to respond.

This is an act of love towards God, yourself, and those around you.

Deuteronomy 28:1-2

> *"¹ If you fully obey the Lord your God and carefully follow all his commands I give you today, the Lord your God will set you high above all the nations on earth. ² All these blessings will come on you and accompany you if you obey the Lord your God."*

James 1:25 NIV

> *²⁵ But whoever looks intently into the perfect law that gives freedom, and continues in it — not forgetting what they have heard, but doing it — they will be blessed in what they do.*

One day, I was scrolling online and saw a question that I've seen many times before. On this particular day, though, the question jumped out at me, and I was flooded with deep revelations about its meaning. I was so overwhelmed that I began to cry.   It simply said, "Are you living buried or planted"? What I saw in my mind was a baseball and a seed buried in the ground. When something is buried, it's in complete darkness. This darkness represents the painful moments in our lives. A baseball will never leave that dark place on its own unless someone digs it up. Its darkness is potentially permanent.

The seed was right next to the baseball. They were both in the same darkness. But the seed will eventually rise up to see light again because it's planted. When something is planted, that means someone is intentionally nurturing it. The person who planted it is making sure it gets water and sunlight and is cared for. That's what life is like when we have God. We can be in the same place of pain caused by the same types of trauma as anyone else. But we have the hope of knowing that someone is pouring into us with the intention of us blooming into something more beautiful than before. The seed knows it will bloom, it doesn't have to question if the darkness is permanent. Once the seed blooms, it will be stronger, wiser, and more equipped for its calling and purpose. It's knowing in your heart that your pain will not be in vain, and this is only for a season.

I then looked back at the baseball. It made me wonder how many people are living buried and hopeless. How many people believe their pain could be permanent? I remember feeling that way for a moment, and I asked myself what I would have been willing to do if I truly believed there was no way out of this pain. It made me understand why so many turn to drugs or alcohol. It's a desperation for anything that can momentarily numb the pain that you believe may be never-ending. This is what led me to start crying. My heart broke for all those who don't know they have a choice to live planted instead of being buried.   All it takes to go from buried to planted is one second of crying out "Jesus". That one name, that one word, can take you from buried to planted in an instant. This vision of the baseball developed a deeper compassion for those who have hurt me. It also made it much easier to choose to love. I choose to love because I now understand that hurt people act out of desperation. I pray this book finds its way to anyone who's living buried, and it guides your path towards blooming.

One thing I want to make very clear is that choosing to forgive and love doesn't mean accepting abuse or disrespect. Some people need to be loved from a distance, and your safety is the priority. You can pray for someone and choose to forgive them without any interaction. A great resource that helped me tremendously in this area was Lysa TerKeurst's books "Forgiving What You

Can't Forget" and "Good Boundaries and
Goodbyes".

Chapter 7

My Role in Healing: Choosing Joy

During my years of intense research, I noticed James 1:2-4 kept popping up everywhere. It would be in the sermons and podcasts I listened to while driving to work. It showed up in books I was reading. It was coming up so much that I was getting annoyed because I felt like whoever wrote this never experienced the betrayal of a family member or spouse. Let's look at what this verse says.

James 1:2-4 NIV

> *2 Consider it pure joy, my brothers and sisters, whenever you face trials of many kinds, 3 because you know that the testing of your faith produces perseverance. 4Let perseverance finish its work so that you may be mature and complete, not lacking anything.*

I knew my response of annoyance wasn't rational, so that began my deep dive into the word joy. Clearly, I must be misinterpreting this verse because who would be happy to go through life's hardships? What I found was that my definition of joy did not match biblical joy.

As it turns out, happiness and joy are not the same thing. Happiness is an emotion like sadness or anger related to our circumstances. Happiness is a reaction to events in our lives. Joy is a choice, unrelated to our circumstances. It's a perspective regardless of what you're going through. Joy is having faith based on choosing to believe God's Word more than your feelings. Choosing joy doesn't mean we don't hurt, feel sad, or get angry; it means we don't let emotions keep us hostage. It's choosing to remember that there's light at the end of the tunnel and God will heal and redeem. It's the feeling of living planted, even when you may still be in the dark phase and can't see the light yet. It's knowing your pain will not be in vain because He promises to make it all work for good. Joy can exist without the desire to smile. Joy can exist with tears because it's an internal choice of hope for what's to come. Let's reread the verse again now with this new understanding.

James 1:2-4 NIV

> [2] *Consider it pure joy, my brothers and sisters, whenever you face trials of many kinds, [3]because you know that the testing of your faith produces perseverance. [4]Let perseverance finish its work so that you may be mature and complete, not lacking anything.*

We can now understand that "consider it pure joy" doesn't refer to the emotion of happiness. It means we get to live in the hope and anticipation of the good He will bring forth. In John 16:33, we read that trouble will come our way, but we can have peace because of the joy of the Lord.

John 16:33 NIV

> [33]"I have told you these things, so that in me you may have peace. In this world, you will have trouble. But take heart! I have overcome the world."

During this period of healing, I purchased a necklace that says "choose joy," and I wore it every day. I saw it every time I looked in the mirror, and it reminded me to live in hope. I highly recommend this. I found one for under $10 online. That necklace was such a reminder that it helped to ease the triggers and panic attacks I was experiencing. It helped to remind me not to let my mind run wild.

Chapter 8

God's Role in Healing

Restore/Heal

The Lord will restore us when we choose to live planted and not buried. Restoration could mean being forgiven and restoring our connection with Him. Restoration can be complete healing physically, mentally, and emotionally. In the case of dealing with trauma, we can trust that He will restore us mentally and emotionally to complete wholeness. This wholeness should be rooted in knowing who you are in Him and walking every day in the confidence of your true worth. He can restore what's been broken or stolen. He can restore strength and guide our feet back to the path of righteousness.

Psalm 147:3 NIV

3He heals the brokenhearted and binds up their wounds.

1 Peter 5:10 NIV

10And the God of all grace, who called you to His eternal Glory in Christ, after you have suffered a little while, will Himself restore you and make you strong, firm, and steadfast.

Psalm 30:2 NIV

2Lord my God, I called to you for help, and you healed me.

Comfort

The Lord promises to comfort us whenever we need. He will give us peace and calm our mind if we just spend time in His presence. We can find comfort by reading the Word, which uplifts us. He sends the Holy Spirit and other believers to comfort us. Praise and worship will also bring us comfort. I personally found worship to be the biggest source of comfort. I sang songs of worship while doing the dishes, cleaning the house, crying, or exercising. There were also times when I couldn't form the words to sing, so I just listened. That's ok too. The point is to worship whether or not you feel like it, and it will always soothe your soul.

2 Corinthians 1:3-4 NIV

> [3] *Praise be to the God and Father of our Lord Jesus Christ, the Father of compassion and the God of all comfort, [4] who comforts us in all our troubles, so that we can comfort those in any trouble with the comfort we ourselves receive from God.*

Redeem

God's role is to take what sin meant to destroy and turn it around to be used for our good. In chapter 3, we spoke about why these things happen. I want to make it clear that God is not the source of the evil things that happen to us.

But He does promise to thwart the enemy's plans and use them for a greater purpose. God's role here is to redeem. He will make it so our pain is not in vain, and He gets the Glory.

Jeremiah 29:11 NIV

> *[11]For I know the plans I have for you," declares the LORD, "plans to prosper you and not to harm you, plans to give you hope and a future.*

Romans 8:28 NIV

> *[28]And we know that in all things God works for the good of those who love Him, who have been called according to his purpose.*

I'm a big jigsaw puzzle person, and it's what I picture when I think of redemption. Imagine a 1,000-piece puzzle. When fully assembled, all the pieces form a beautiful picture. I look at events in our lives as individual puzzle pieces that will form a picture at the end of our time here. I believe when we live for God, He will orchestrate all the pieces/events to form a masterpiece. You'll see that everything was perfectly connected to reflect a life that helped enrich His kingdom. Our fruit will be seen throughout the entire picture. That's what will make the completed puzzle of our lives a masterpiece and not just a pretty picture. He'll orchestrate it all to have divine purpose.

On judgment day, I believe God will show us our completed puzzle. We'll see whether we assembled the pieces ourselves or trusted Him to do it. It will reveal how our obedience or disobedience shaped what he could create. This means trusting Him to guide your steps when you're blinded by pain. That means trusting when you're unable to see the purpose. The enemy may sneak a couple of unwanted pieces into the puzzle through sin, but God will redeem those events. He'll arrange even those pieces to perfectly fit into the puzzle and make it even more beautiful.

Let's choose to live in the hope of believing our God sees every tear and will keep His promises to restore, heal, comfort, and redeem.

Chapter 9

Your Brain's Role in Healing

During my research on healing, I learned that trauma has a great impact on the brain. I became curious about what that meant and if there's anything I could do to influence that impact. I started to read every article and study I could find on this topic. There were several key actions I implemented in my life that definitely helped the healing process along.

The first thing I learned, which was a big shocker, is that trauma actually changes the structure and chemistry of our brains. This alteration affects the ability to have rational thoughts and reactions. It also causes irrational physical reactions, which is why I was having triggers, panic attacks, and chest pains for a period of time. You may permanently feel unsafe because of a perceived danger that you're not really in. During these reactions to trauma, our body releases stress hormones such as adrenaline and cortisol, which trigger a fast heartbeat, quickened breathing, and high blood pressure.

The good news I found is that our brain can be healed, and we can play a role in helping that healing along. Ever hear of neuroplasticity? Well, neither had I. Neuroplasticity is the brain's ability to rewire and reorganize itself with new neural connections. Our brain can form new connections and pathways through practices we can implement in our lives. These are new pathways of healing based on the practices we'll talk about, and of which I personally implemented.

Gratitude

Gratitude activates the brain's reward system and releases neurotransmitters such as serotonin and dopamine. Serotonin triggers feelings of happiness, contentment, and peace. Dopamine triggers feelings of pleasure and reward. The more you practice gratitude, the more you'll produce serotonin and dopamine. Practicing gratitude over time will rewire your brain for the better. You're basically training your brain to better handle its emotions and stresses. In Chapter 4, we discussed why biblically we need to practice Thanksgiving. Science calls it gratitude. So not only does God's word say gratefulness is healing, but so does science. There are hundreds of studies connecting a grateful attitude to rewiring the brain for healing.

Movement

Dopamine is also released when you do things like exercising, walking, biking, gardening, spending time in nature, and participating in hobbies. We have a choice to live a life that naturally promotes more dopamine and neuroplasticity, leading to healing. This is another practice I implemented right away.

Where I live, we have a beautiful walking/bike path. There's a stretch of the path with very tall trees on both sides. The trees arch towards the center and create a canopy over the path, but they also allow stunning sunlight to shine through. It's breathtaking. I was never a walker because of the medical issues I mentioned earlier with my feet. But I figured out how much walking I could manage and started walking 5 days a week. Every time I walked, it felt therapeutic and healing. I became excited about my time walking outdoors and looked forward to it. The feeling of the sun on my face and the vibrant colors of the leaves all boosted my mood. I did this for about 6 months while the weather was warm enough, and I can tell you with absolute honesty that it drastically sped up my healing. It wasn't just the act of exercising outdoors; it was also the fact that I was practicing self-care.

Healthy Diet and Hydration

You probably won't be surprised by this next action. A healthy diet and hydration impact the brain's ability to function properly. We should be eating whole grains, vegetables, lean meat, and limiting processed foods. The right foods will help your brain heal by providing the vitamins and minerals it needs. A poor diet consists of sugary drinks, refined carbohydrates, and processed foods. These types of foods have been linked to inflammation, poor brain function, and depression. My personal approach is to eat mostly whole foods. Whole foods don't have a list of ingredients on its packaging. For example, meat, potatoes, and vegetables are in their whole natural state and do not have a list of ingredients on their packaging.

Hydration supports neuroplasticity, so the brain can form new pathways. The brain is made up of 75% water. Dehydration can negatively impact the brain's ability to function and heal. I paired my daily walk with hydration and a healthy diet. I aimed for about 75-100 ounces of water a day. My goal here was mainly to promote the healing of my brain from the trauma, but I also ended up losing almost 15lbs!

Journaling

Journaling is a healthy way to release your feelings. Journaling is another way to rewire your brain and strengthen the new pathways. Writing your feelings down is calming and can improve your mood. You don't have to only write about your feelings. My journal was mostly filled with what I was learning. Every time I heard an interesting fact or an uplifting message, I wrote it in the journal. I made it a point to read something in the journal every day. My memory isn't that great, so I forget what I hear or read very quickly. Being able to go back to the journal was very refreshing. It uplifted me on the hard days and renewed my hope. If you decide to start a journal, include anything in this book that stood out to you. I made a list of all the scientific actions (walking, exercising, gratitude, healthy diet, journaling, and partaking in hobbies), and I would refer to the list and make sure I acted on most of them every day. This book will only help if you remember to take the steps of action.

Community

If you're really struggling, I suggest seeking professional help from a counselor or therapist. Professionals are trained to help rewire your brain for healing. I also sought my own counseling during this time. My biggest fear was letting this turn me into someone I wasn't meant to be. The counseling really helped with that.

You'll also benefit from spending extra time with friends. Whether it is through a counselor or friends, the point is not to isolate.

Your initial reaction may be to hold everything inside because you don't want others to know. You may feel embarrassed or believe it's your fault. Betrayal is not your fault. I remember a stage where I didn't want to ever leave the house. I thought as long as I'm not around anyone, no one can betray or hurt me. Thank God that only lasted a short time. I quickly learned that isolation hinders healing.   I made plans to hangout with friends, go to the movies, host dinner parties, and have game nights. Even though I was sad all the time, these interactions allowed for moments of fun and laughter. I made the effort to be present during these times and fully enjoy making new memories. It allowed me to have periods of relief from sadness. Each interaction healed me a little bit more.

I encourage you to invest in yourself. Push yourself to implement some of these suggestions. For me, walking had the biggest impact on my mental health. Find what works best for you and stick with it daily.

Chapter 10

Conclusion

If this book made its way into your hands, know that I'm praying for you. I'm hoping you've been able to underline, highlight, or bookmark some of the actionable steps you want to implement. Make a list and keep it somewhere you can view daily. I pray you're able to quickly get your footing on the path to healing and walk it confidently. It's a hard road, but just start by putting one foot in front of the other. Choose to live planted along the journey. Choose the joy of the Lord in anticipation of blooming. Choose forgiveness to free up space in your heart for healing. Choose obedience in spite of your feelings. Choose to do it God's way in every moment and watch what He'll be able to accomplish in your life and those around you.

The pain will eventually subside, and you'll have a powerful testimony that impacts eternity.

Enjoyed This Book? Your Review Really Helps

If this book helped you in any way, I'd be incredibly grateful if you could take a minute to leave a short review on Amazon.

Thank you for your time and support,

Shanna Foster

Acknowledgements

Books

Bait of Satan - John Bevere

Good Boundaries and Goodbyes - Lysa TerKeurst

How to Forgive What You Can't Forget - Lysa TerKeurst

It's Not Supposed to Be This Way - Lysa TerKeurst

Love Like You've Never Been Hurt - Jentezen Franklin

Websites

Duomo.com - Unhealthy Relationship Patterns Bible Healing Plan

Podcasts

Tony Evans' Podcast

Joyce Meyers - 15 Minutes in the Word with Joyce

Jimmy & Karen Evans - Marriage Today

Rick Warren - Pastor Rick's Daily Hope

ABOUT THE AUTHOR

Shanna N Foster, a native to New York is Pace University graduate with a Masters in Computer Information Systems. She has been a member of the Yorktown Assembly of God church in Yorktown Heights, NY for more than 20 years. She teaches multiple adult Bible studies through her church and has a personal ministry in helping women heal from the painful moments of life. She has 2 school-aged children. She understands the pain of being betrayed by family members as well as her spouse. Through years of research and personal application she has learned how God wants us to handle these times in our lives.

Author's website:

https://sites.google.com/view/shannanfoster